Business in Minutes

Business in Minutes

How To Profit From The On-Demand Revolution

Jim Spavins

This publication is designed to provide competent and reliable information regarding the subject matter covered. However, it is sold with the understanding that the author and publisher are not engaged in rendering legal, medical, financial, or other professional advice.

Although based on a true story, certain events in the book have been fictionalized for educational content and impact.

Copyright © 2010 by Isthmus Ventures, LLC
All rights reserved.

No part of this book may be used or reproduced in any manner whatsoever without written permission, except in the case of brief quotations embodied in critical articles or reviews.

Published 2010

Printed by Create Space in the United States of America

ISBN: 1450599060

ISBN-13: 9781450599061

Business in Minutes
Table of Contents

Introduction 11

The Business Model 19

Market Research 31

Revenue Sources 43

Marketing and Sales Plan 57

Create Your Products 73

Build Your Web Presence 85

Evaluate Your Results 99

Growing Your Business 109

Are you ready? 119

Quick Start Checklist 125

Example Business Plan 127

Additional Reading 137

On-Demand Websites 139

Acknowledgements

My name may be on the front cover but I would be remiss if I did not thank all my friends, colleagues, classmates, and professors at the University of Wisconsin-Madison's MBA program. Their influence can be found throughout the book and I appreciate all the time they let me bend their ears and discuss the ideas found here. In my mind, this group of people is second to none in their business acumen and passion to do great things.

CHAPTER 1

Introduction

Chapter 1
Introduction

If you could spend your day doing anything you want, what would you do? What is that one thing that will make you jump out of bed early in the morning and stay up until late into the night? The answer to this question is your passion. What would you do if I told you there was a way to turn that passion, with little additional time or monetary investment, into a part time business that will provide you with passive income?

If you have ever had the passing thought of taking your passion and building a business, all the tools you will need to build a world class business with valuable products are just a few keystrokes away. The early 21st century has seen the rise of companies that allow individuals the opportunity to create products and sell to the mass market, on-demand without the need to purchase inventory, fill orders, or ship the products. These companies' on-demand service produces products only when a customer makes a purchase.

As an individual with a passion, this is a very exciting change. If you can determine the best way to turn your passion into content, you can build a business in minutes. The on-demand companies will allow you, a passionate content creator, the opportunity to make products and sell them to the world directly. There is no longer a need to work through gatekeepers, such as book publishers, record companies, or film production companies, to have your product reach a customer.

What this also means is that those with an interest in building a small part time business providing content to a niche market is now just a few minutes away. There is no need to decide whether or not to fund the 401(k) or invest in a part time business. The startup costs for a business developed around these on-demand tools are now essentially zero. Not so long ago, if an individual had a passion and wanted to create products to sell, it meant having to purchase a large quantity of inventory of his product with the hope of one day being able to sell them all to recoup his initial investment.

The on-demand model is simply a shift in the distribution model and who holds the inventory risk. No longer does the content creator need to either convince a publishing company, record label, or retail store to carry their content. Instead, the creator can make their product and bring it directly to consumers through online stores.

While the elimination of these barriers to entry is great for the individual, it also means that anyone else with the motivation to create content can enter too. This makes the competition fierce. It requires passion and follow through when you build your business or else you will not survive.

This on-demand business model offers tremendous financial possibilities for the enterprising content creator. By using just a small collection of on-demand providers, you can build a business that delivers multiple revenue streams with minimal cost and investment.

This book will help those with a passion harness the power of the on-demand model and organize a profitable business model, develop a successful marketing and sales plan, produce quality products, and create a powerful web presence. In particular, each chapter will focus on the following areas:

- ✓ The Business Model

How will you make money? How much will it cost? What is the initial investment? All of these questions will be answered with the business model for the on-demand business.

- ✓ Market Research

You have the greatest idea for a product since the invention of sliced bread, but who will buy it? There is a big difference between creating a great product and creating a great product that people will buy. Researching your market will be a key to the success of your business.

- ✓ Revenue Sources

There are numerous providers of on-demand businesses. Which will provide the best service for you? The Revenue Sources chapter will provide an overview of services offered by several different companies and how best to use them.

- ✓ Sales and Marketing Plan

One of the key differentiators in your business will be how you plan to market it. Without a plan in place, you will not be able to survive for long. Your success will depend upon your ability to put in place the correct strategy.

- ✓ Creating Your Products

Once you have a plan in place, it is time to roll up your sleeves and get to work. If you have no idea how to create your products, this chapter will help you get started whether it is a book, CD, DVD, or graphics.

- ✓ Building Your Web Presence

Don't know the difference between coffee and Java? That's ok. You can still get everything online and looking great without a master's degree in computer science.

✓ Evaluating Your Business

Once you have everything up and running, how will you know if you are reaching your goals? Also, how will you receive customer feedback? Collecting and analyzing this data is important for your long term success.

✓ Growing Your Business

Do you want to take your small on-demand business and build a sustainable enterprise? You will need to put a sustainable plan together to take your startup to world domination.

At the end of every chapter, there is a case study section called "Business at Work." In each of these sections you will follow an example business that was run for over a year with the on-demand business model. The business is called The Rockville Bridge and focuses on a micro-niche within the hobby of model railroading. The business was designed to serve a small market but show how easy and simple it is to create a part time business that will make money.

You will notice that this example business was meant to provide part time income based on one to two hours a week of working on the business. Does this mean you can't make enough money to use this business model for a full time business? The short answer is no but it will be difficult. This example business was focused on a very small market. If you want to have bigger financial results, you will have to focus on a larger market with more customers.

So, are you ready to take your passion and create a business around it? The answer should be yes. Before reading the next chapter, I want you to take out a piece of paper and at the top of it, write your passion. As you follow along with each chapter, take the time to think about how you can take the lessons and apply them to what you wrote at the top of that page. As you finish the chapter, write down how you will apply it to your business idea. When you reach the end of the book, you will have everything you need to get started. At that point, it will be time to get to work. If you put in the effort and stay disciplined, success can be yours.

CHAPTER 2

The Business Model

Chapter 2
The Business Model

In simple terms, the business model explains how the company makes money, what the costs associated with bringing in revenue, and what investment is needed to make it happen. A successful business model is one that brings in more revenue than it loses in costs and covers the investment in the business. Simple, right?

The on-demand business model that we are going to discuss is fairly straight forward. The revenue sources are all royalties that you will earn when someone actually purchases a product from the on-demand company. There is no inventory to purchase and sell, just content to create which keeps the financial risks low.

Revenues

It should go without saying that you need to figure out how you plan to make money from your business. There are numerous products to generate revenue in the on-demand business space. Here is just a sampling:

- ✓ Books and eBooks
- ✓ CDs (Audio and Data)

- ✓ DVDs (Video and Data)
- ✓ Apparel
- ✓ Posters
- ✓ Bumper Stickers
- ✓ Buttons
- ✓ Canvas Artwork
- ✓ Calendars
- ✓ Photographs

This is just a small sampling and in Chapter 4, we will highlight specific companies and what they offer. In addition to products, since this book will focus on building a web based business, you can also consider some other web based revenue sources such as:

- ✓ Display Advertising
- ✓ Affiliate Commissions

While these last two ideas can certainly add to the bottom line, they are also some of the hardest to grow to large numbers. Unless you think that you can build traffic to your main website to the tens of thousands of visitors a day, the revenue from advertising and affiliates will be small. The ads on your site also have the potential to distract from what you are trying to sell, which is your on-demand product.

Whichever products you choose, a successful on-demand business should have multiple streams of revenue. This means that you will not rely on just one product for all of your sales. For example, if you are an author and have a book, are there any other products that can create a synergy with book sales? It's important to keep this in mind as you develop your plan.

Costs

The nice part of an on-demand business model is that your fixed costs are relatively low. Generally, if you are planning on keeping things at a small scale, these expenses will be limited to such items as web hosting and domain name renewal. Since with this model you will not need to carry any inventory, this will make every sale of a product a variable expense. If no one makes a purchase, you have no inventory expense.

One of the expenses you may decide to incur is advertising expense. This will certainly allow you to reach a larger audience faster than if you try many organic word-of-mouth strategies; however it will be more expensive. In Chapter 5, we will discuss some ideas on how to minimize this expense.

One of the final costs you will want to incur is to purchase proof copies of your products. It is best to actually try the on-demand services you wish to use to make sure that it meets all of your requirements from quality to customer service. In fact, some of the companies require that you purchase a proof copy before you even begin to sell your items.

Investment

With such low fixed costs, it also means your initial investment will also be low. Ideally, you should be able to self fund this venture out of your own pocket. Realistically, you will at most spend a few hundred dollars getting the business going. If you are anticipating spending more, evaluate your expenses to see if they will result in more sales.

Generally, some of the initial investments that you will have to spend money on might include:

- ✓ Software Purchases
- ✓ Incorporation Expenses
- ✓ Graphic Design Services
- ✓ Web Design and Programming
- ✓ Domain Purchases
- ✓ Web Hosting Services

There may be more or less depending upon what resources you already have access to as well as what skills you bring to the table.

What are the disadvantages?

With all of the positives that have been outlined about the business model, it is fair to point out that there are some disadvantages that may prove to be weaknesses in your business if you fail to take them into account.

Low Risk = Low Return

Anyone who has spent some time studying finance understands the principal that risk and return are related. If you don't take much risk, you will have small returns (both small gains and small losses). If you take big risks, you can make big returns as well as big losses. There is very little financial risk to this model which means it can be difficult to make big returns. The potential returns you can earn will be determined by the size of your potential market, the quality of your products, as well as your marketing and sales plan. As we will discuss throughout the book, it may be possible to quit your day job, just don't make an appointment to visit the Ferrari dealer anytime soon.

Barriers to Entry

With so little upfront costs, it should come as no surprise that there are also no barriers to entry for a competitor to build a competing business with a similar idea. Everyone with an internet connection has access to the same technology as you. The only differentiation you will ever have is your brand and content. Be very aware of this fact and understand that you will always have competitors. This is also one of the reasons I strongly suggest that it would be difficult to leave your day job and make this a full time business. However, you can still make money without much effort and doing something you would do anyway.

Other Things to Consider

If you are serious about creating a sustainable business, there are some other very important things to consider before jumping in with both feet.

- ✓ Decide to incorporate

The structure of the on-demand service providers is that you will receive royalty money for giving them a license to print or publish your content. This makes a corporation unnecessary unless you want to deduct any expenses related to your business from your taxes or you would like to reduce your personal liability. A corporation will allow you to do both. Starting a corporation will result in more costs, such as filing fees and annual state franchise taxes but will reduce your personal liability and separate your business from your private activities. If you do decide to go in that direction, you will need to pick an organizational type such as a sole proprietorship, Limited Liability Company, Limited Liability Partnership, S-Corp, or a C-corp. Each has its own advantages, disadvantages, and costs. This is beyond the scope of this book, but if you have dreams of building a business beyond the on-demand model, it's best to start on the right foot and incorporate early in the process.

If you do decide to incorporate, each state has information on how to incorporate along with the paperwork you will need to file. Generally, the Secretary of the State is responsible for this activity within the state and you will be able to find the information on their website.

Once you have all of your state paperwork filled out, you will need to obtain a Federal Employer ID number. You will also want to setup a separate business bank account to keep all of your financial transactions and paperwork separate from your personal finances.

- ✓ Hire an Attorney and CPA

Before you jump right in and start building everything, you will want to talk to a lawyer and a Certified Public Accountant (CPA). If you are planning on building a business empire, it is best to find the right attorney and CPA before you make it big. They will be able to help guide you through some legal landmines that could be waiting for you as well as make sure your accounting systems are in place in case the IRS comes calling for an audit. You should be able to have a free introductory meeting to learn about the services they provide and how much their services costs.

- ✓ Write a Business Plan

This is required no matter what business structure you decide on. Now, I know the idea of writing a business plan strikes fear into many potential entrepreneurs but it allows you an opportunity to clearly think through what you are going to do and how you plan to accomplish it. A business plan for this style of business does not need to be long or complicated but it's still important. At the end of the book in the Resources section, you will find a sample business plan for The Rockville Bridge business. As you will see, it is only eight pages long but covers all the key areas for producing a successful strategy.

- ✓ Pick a name

The final step is to pick a name for your business. You will need to check and see if this name is already taken by another business by searching the businesses registered within the state which you are operating as well as the US Patent and Trademark office. Also, you will want to purchase the domain name as soon as possible. If the domain is already taken, there is a good chance someone may have already registered a business in that name too.

Case Study

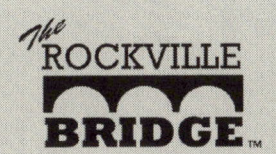

Business at Work

The ROCKVILLE BRIDGE™

The Rockville Bridge business was designed to produce content that would be valuable to model railroaders and railroad enthusiasts who are interested in modeling stone bridges. The highlights include information about the world's longest stone masonry arch bridge called Rockville Bridge located near Harrisburg, PA. This landmark is well known among railroad enthusiasts and many travel to see the bridge. The business would focus its efforts on providing information about the bridge and how to build scale models of it.

Revenue Sources

In order to generate revenue, the business focuses on three revenue sources: book sales, product sales, and advertising. The book is a how-to guide for model railroaders interested in building a model of the bridge. The products include t-shirts with the Rockville Bridge logo, a coffee mug with the same logo, an apron, and postcards with a photo of a train on the bridge. Advertising revenue comes from Google Adsense and the Amazon affiliates program. The Google Adsense program provides display ads that produce revenue based on the number of page views and clicks on the ads. The Amazon affiliates program pays a commission when someone clicks from The Rockville Bridge website and purchases an item.

Expenses

To keep the business up and running, there are very few expenses. The main web site requires web hosting and a domain name. These are fixed, annual expenses. The only other expenses that are incurred are some printing expenses for flyers and proof copies of books and products. These are all variable expenses.

Investment

So just how much cash is needed to get a very small project like this up and running? The answer is very little. The first purchase was of the domain name and web hosting. This bill totaled just under $75 for one year. As we will discuss in later chapters, products need to be designed, logos created, and websites built. Depending upon your unique skills, you may or may not need to pay other people to do them. This cost needs to be added to your initial investment. For this project, I was able to accomplish all those tasks on my own. However, this did take a fair amount of time – approximately 40 hours – so it will be important to take this into account when evaluating the results of this business in Chapter 9.

CHAPTER 3

Market Research

Chapter 3
Market Research

Before you dig in and start designing your products, authoring that book, or filming the next big documentary, you need to figure out if there is anyone out there who will be interested in purchasing it! Your friends and family may love what you do, but that is a very small market and a tough one to survive with.

After producing a quality product and having a sound marketing and sales plan, market research should be a mandatory step you take before you launch your business. Before you plan your product, you should be able to answer the following questions:

- ✓ Who is your customer?
- ✓ How many potential customers are there?
- ✓ How does your customer shop?
- ✓ How easy is it for you to reach your potential customers?
- ✓ What value will your customers receive from your product?

Once you have the answers to these questions, you will be able to make better judgments on how to design your products and set up your marketing and sales plan. Let's break down how to answer each of these questions.

Who is your customer?

It is fundamentally important to understand the demographic information behind who your customer is. This will influence the words you use on your website and marketing materials, the color choices, fonts, logo designs, and even the products you create.

Think about these questions as they relate to your potential customer. Is your customer male or female or both? How old are they? How much money do they make? Where do they live? Does the customer use the product you want to create? If you can answer these questions you will have a better idea of how to approach your business. You may also learn that your business idea may not work with the group that you want to reach. Your product idea may be too expensive or the wrong colors. When you have a good idea of who would be interested in purchasing your product, keep this information filed away until it is time to start designing your product and putting together the marketing and sales plan.

How many potential customers are there?

No matter how great a product you make or how sound your marketing and sales plan is, you will not be able to make a lot of revenue if the market is tiny. When researching to determine your total market size, be careful in your data selection and assumptions. Remember that even some of the biggest and best known brands in the world do not reach 100% of their total market.

How does your customer shop?

Since the idea behind this business model is that you exclusively sell your products on the internet, your customers must also shop there. This is critical because if you are targeting a market where the customer does not regularly use the internet to purchase the product you are selling, you will have difficulty changing their behavior to match your sales channel.

Let's look at an example. Say you want to make t-shirts with funny slogans on them for men over 65 years old. How many men over 65 use the internet to buy their clothing? I don't think we have to put together a fancy marketing research study to tell us that the number of customers would be small compared to the population of men over the age of 65. This does not mean that the business would not generate sales or that there are no customers, it is just a much smaller number than the entire group.

How easy is it for you to reach your potential customers?

It is important to think about where your customers are and what they do. Think about these specific questions:

- ✓ Are there specific websites that they go to regularly?
- ✓ Are there places that they go?
- ✓ Are there particular television shows or radio stations that they listen to?
- ✓ Are there magazines that they subscribe to?
- ✓ Are there particular organizations that they join?

Why is this important? This will help you determine the best way to reach your potential customers to tell them first that you exist, and second the products you are offering. It will also determine how much it might cost you, in either time or money, to reach them. This will be an important piece of the marketing and sales plan later so you have to find out where they are.

What value do you add?

At the end of the day, you need to make a product that your customer will value is some way. It may be financial or it may be intangible but you have to deliver that value to them. Remember, you have to convince the customer that what you have available is worth enough for them to pull out their wallet, take out their credit card, fill out an order form, and wait a few days for the product to show up at their door step.

Let's use this book as a concrete example of a product that will add value. If you have this in your hands, you paid $19.95 plus shipping and handling with the idea that it would show you how to build an on-demand business and that you could make your $19.95 plus shipping and handling back. Right? If you do build a business following the ideas in this book and make more than $19.95 plus shipping and handling, it has added value to you. If not, then it didn't add value.[1] That's a harsh example but the idea is correct. Ultimately your customers will be the judge of whether the products you offer have enough value to them to purchase them from you.

Where to find data

Asking the questions was the easy part; actually finding the answers is the difficult part. This is one of the reasons why there are many highly paid market research professionals who work every day to learn about customers for companies. Since this book

---

[1] This book could also have some intangible value to you if you don't use it to build a business like the one described but helped you in another way.

focuses on simpler solutions and does not expect anyone to fund a complete market study, we will offer some ideas that will help you get a rough idea of the market you are interested in selling to.

- ✓ US Census Data – Every 10 years, the United States government conducts a census to count the population of the country. In addition, it collects a treasure trove of additional data about what people do in their leisure time, how they travel, and numerous other data points. Take a look at their website and scroll through the data. This will give you some broad based numbers to work from. However, if you are looking at a smaller niche market, you will need to find other sources.
- ✓ Organizational Memberships – If your idea focuses on a particular trade group or hobby, there generally are organizations that people can join. These organizations sometimes have basic demographic information available or at least the total number of members. This can give you some base numbers to work from.
- ✓ Magazine Subscribers – Just like with organizations, these people have paid to stay up to date on a particular interest. If you think you might want to advertise with one of these magazines, call their advertising department. Most have advertising kits that include all

kinds of demographic information about their readers.
- ✓ Talk to potential customers – If your idea is your passion, chances are you already know a couple of people who might be interested in what you are doing as well. Take the time to discuss the idea with them. This type of secondary research might help you understand a bit more about how easy it will be to reach your customer, how they shop, and what value will you add to them. Just remember that you might have some blinders on about your passion and think that everyone that is also interested in the same passion will want to purchase your product. This will not be the case which makes discussing it all the more important.

It is essential to remember that these numbers you will come up with are estimates only and not fact. It is also important to remember that you will not achieve sales to 100%.

Top Down versus Bottom Up Market Analysis

Much of the data that you will find in answering the questions listed at the start of the chapter will give you a good look at the market from the top down. This means that you will understand what the entire potential market for your product can be. However, there is another critical factor in evaluating your market and that is from the bottom up. This is essential for looking at the planned operations of your business and its ability to serve that market. For example is it a large diverse group or a highly targets, tight knit community. This will determine how much time and effort it will take to reach your intended customer market.

One of the great ideas behind the on-demand business model is that it frees your time from having to deal with inventory and filling orders. This makes this type of business an ideal part time endeavor. If you choose to run your business in that fashion, chances are you will not be able to as effectively serve a large market as well as if you worked on the business full time. Think about everything you will still need to do. You will still have to spend time marketing your business, answering questions, maintaining your websites and social networks, as well as cashing all those royalty checks. Even the products geared at the largest of markets will still take effort to get the word out to everyone. This is an important factor in determining your bottom up market analysis.

Case Study

Business at Work

The ROCKVILLE BRIDGE™

So just who are the customers who would buy a book about a stone masonry arch bridge in Pennsylvania?

Top Down Market Analysis

First let's find out the market size. The easiest categories to look at for some practical numbers are the number of people subscribing to magazines and belonging to national organizations. In the world of model railroading, the major organization of hobbyists is the National Model Railroad Association (NMRA) which consists of 20,000 members. The larger magazines have circulations in the 100,000s. While certainly not every hobbyist belongs to this organization or subscribes to those magazines, it is a starting point. However this is the entire model railroad market and not everyone will be interested in this particular book. We need to find those interested in the railroads of Pennsylvania. For this we will look at some of the smaller organizations and in this case there is the Pennsylvania Railroad Historical Society. Membership is only several thousand strong. Even within this group, not everyone will be book consumers but we are getting closer. At this point, we will make an educated guess that there may be up to

1000 potential customers for this book based on this top down analysis.

Bottom Up Market Analysis

One of the problems with the top down analysis is that it looks at the total potential market. However, how long will it take you to reach them all? How much will this cost either in your time or advertising money? How many books would need to be sold a day to sell one to every person in that market?

Let's take a look at the proposed operations for the company outlined in the business plan. The idea behind this business is that only one to two hours a week is spent working on the business and no money would be spent on paid advertising. Over the course of the year, only 50 hours would be spent marketing the business. To sell 1000 books, I'd have to sell 20 per hour! That is probably not realistic. What is more likely is that I might be able to generate a couple of sales an hour. (Of course, I am assuming there are no direct sales for bulk orders to a retail store or book dealer which could be an option).

So the top down analysis tells us that there is a potential customer base of approximately 1000 customers for this type of book while the bottom up analysis says that we might only sell 100 copies. Check back for the results in Chapter 9.

CHAPTER 4

Revenue Sources

Chapter 4
Revenue Sources

Now that you have done your market research and understand your market, it is time to determine which on-demand companies will provide the products that you want to sell. In this chapter is a listing of companies that offer on-demand services. Each is unique and offers slightly different options. We will only look at four companies that offer services with no or small setup costs. There are others that require a setup fee (generally in the hundreds to thousands of dollars).

Before plunging in head first, take some time to research each company's offerings and potentially order a test product to see if it meets your expectations. Remember, you need to make sure the quality and delivery of the products is the best it can possibly be. You are hiring these companies as contractors to bring your content to life. You should not settle until you have found what you are looking for.

Some of the factors you should consider when selecting a company are as follows:

- ✓ Customer experience – How user-friendly are the store fronts? What are the payment

options? Are directions easy to follow? Are the graphics clean and sharp?
- ✓ Product quality – What materials are used? Is the printing in focus?
- ✓ Customer service –What is the method of support? Email? Live chat? Phone? How quick is the response?
- ✓ Shipping – What are the shipping options? What are the costs? Does the packaging protect the item during transit?
- ✓ Payment period – How often do they send royalty checks?
- ✓ Customizable – Can you have your own store front? Can you add your own graphics and colors?

In the end, you have to make the decision which is right for what you are trying to sell. The companies listed below all have their advantages and disadvantages depending upon what you want to sell.

On-Demand Products

Over the next several pages you will find detailed information about four of the larger on-demand printing companies. This is not an all inclusive list. These generally show the range of products that you can make with any of these types of companies and how they work. Again, before making your decision, take some time to research your decision.

CaféPress

CaféPress offers a very large selection of customizable items and products that the content creator can place their designs on. All the items have printed graphics so only an image file is required to upload your designs into their system. A user can create a free store front which can be customized with a header graphic and welcome message. In addition, you can upgrade, for a fee, to a storefront without the CaféPress banner across the top of the page allowing your site to seamlessly flow with your store. Below is a partial list of the products that can be customized and sold through a store.

- ✓ Apparel – Mens, Womens, and Kids and Baby products ranging from t-shirts to undergarments.
- ✓ Accessories – Items in this category include bags, totes, hats, aprons, and ties.
- ✓ Household Items – Mugs, mouse pads, calendars, stationary, pillows, and tile coasters.
- ✓ Prints – If you are a photographer or artist you can have your photos printed.
- ✓ Unique Gifts – These are items not listed in the above category and include license plate frames, ornaments, and bumper stickers.
- ✓ Books and CDs

CreateSpace

CreateSpace is part of Amazon and offers on-demand book publishing, CD production, and DVD production. The selling point for using this service is that your product can be listed on Amazon. Obviously, as one of the biggest online retailers in the world, this is a great marketplace to have your products featured. They offer two versions of their service – a free standard plan and a Pro Plan. The Pro Plan costs $39 per item but does offer higher royalties on each item sold. This could be beneficial if you have a hit and sell lots of copies of your book, CD, or DVD.[2]

Below is a list of CreateSpace product offerings:

- ✓ Books – Authors can publish a paperback book in either color or black and white. There is a small selection of industry standard sizes from 6x9 to 8x10 books. All authors receive an ISBN for their book.
- ✓ CDs – For the musician, audio CDs are offered. There is no option for data CDs so software creators are out of luck.
- ✓ DVDs – If you make movies, video DVDs are offered. Again, no data DVDs are available.

---

[2] In the interest of full disclosure, this book is printed by CreateSpace and the author has several other titles available with the company.

Lulu

If you are looking to sell any type of printed medium, then Lulu may be your one stop shop. Lulu offers a huge range of printed book options (paperback, hardcover, spiral bound, and more) as well as calendars, CDs and DVDs. Lulu offers a free storefront for content creators so if you have multiple titles or items for sale, they are all in one place. In addition, you do have the option to obtain an ISBN and have your product considered for distribution on Amazon and several other online retail booksellers.

Below are some of the Lulu product offerings:

- ✓ Books – Lulu offers one of the most complete printing options for authors. Books can be printed in either black and white or color. In addition, books can be published in either hardcover or paperback versions. Authors have the option of obtaining an ISBN but not all book sizes are eligible for this service.
- ✓ CDs – If you have a product that will work on CD, you can create it through Lulu. Unlike CreateSpace, CDs can have any file format desired so you could sell software or a slideshow.
- ✓ DVDs – Just like CDs, DVDs can have any file format placed on them.

Zazzle

Just like CaféPress, Zazzle offers a wide range of customizable products. Many of the items are similar such as the apparel and accessories category. However, there are some different products offered and embroidery on-demand is offered if you are interested in a higher quality polo shirt instead of t-shirt.

Just like CaféPress, a user can create their own store that can be customized to match the look and feel of their own website. Below is a listing of just some of the items that can be sold in a Zazzle store.

- ✓ Apparel – Mens, Womens, and Kids and Baby products ranging from t-shirts to undergarments.
- ✓ Accessories – Items in this category include bags, totes, hats, aprons, and ties.
- ✓ Household Items – Mugs, mouse pads, calendars, stationary, pillows, and tile coasters.
- ✓ Prints – If you are a photographer or artist you can have your photos printed.
- ✓ Unique Gifts – These are items not listed in the above category and include key chains, magnets, skateboards, and bumper stickers.

Display Advertising

Besides creating products to sell, you can generate additional revenue by displaying ads related to the content on your web site. There are a number of companies that offer an ad network that can be placed on your site. Based upon the traffic to your site and the number clicks on ads, you will receive a payment from advertisers.

Two of the larger companies to offer this service to small scale website publishers are Google Adsense and Yahoo Publisher Network. Both systems are similar in how a website owner goes about placing ads on their site. The first step is to create an account. Both have an approval process to ensure your website matches the terms and conditions that are generally quick, a few days at most. Once approved, you will be able to create customized banner ads and links that you can place your site. For each of these customized designs, unique HTML code will be generated and then you place them on your site where you would like the ads to be displayed. If you are not familiar with HTML, don't let this scare you off. We will explain more in Chapter 7. Once the code is placed on your site and active, your site will be crawled for content and appropriate ads will be displayed on your site. This system is very simple and convenient and requires no more work on the part of the website owner. Google and Yahoo take care of selling the ad space and filling it with relevant ads. This is an ideal system if you are truly looking for passive income from your business.

One word of caution about trying to make money by using advertising on your site, unless you plan to have traffic to your website in the tens of thousands of viewers per day, do not expect to make large sums of money through this revenue stream. This is not to say it is not possible, but you will need content that brings a large number of eyeballs to your site every day. In addition, don't forget that by placing advertisers on your site, you are also drawing attention away from what you are trying to sell. Keep this in mind before deciding to add this revenue stream to your business model.

If you are creating content for a small niche segment, you might be able to consider the do-it-yourself approach to display advertising. This is more involved as it will require you to sell advertising space on your site. However, you will receive the full price of the ad spend. Using the Yahoo and Google service, while extremely convenient, does cost you a piece of the money the advertiser spends. Obviously, Google and Yahoo take a percentage to cover their overhead and profit margin.

If you decide to go this route, you will need to be able to show potential advertisers hard data about traffic to your site. You will need to be able to show them how it benefits them by advertising on your site as opposed to taking those dollars elsewhere.

However, this opens up some flexibility on your part as well. You could potentially offer an advertiser an exclusive deal for display ads on your site (generally, the Yahoo and Google ads have text ads for several different advertisers in one ad) and jointly market their service in all of your platforms and channels. Again, this is more work, but you might be able to add many more dollars to your bottom line if you are a small niche content producer.

Affiliate Programs

Another option to display advertising is affiliate programs. Generally, affiliate marketing programs are a commission system where a website owner can earn money by referring visitors to another site where they can make a purchase. The commission varies but is usually a percentage of sales. This can be very lucrative if the potential sale has a high dollar figure.

The advantage to the advertiser compared to display advertising is that they only pay when they have made a sale. This also means that as the website publisher, this is the only time you receive payment as well. This is a tradeoff but if you spend some time looking at the commission offerings you might be able to find some that offer a fairly high dollar value compared to what you might be able to achieve by just offering display advertising.

For example, if you have a site that focuses on travel, there are several travel and tourism companies like hotel chain and rental car companies that offer affiliate programs where as the referring website, you make a percentage of the sale (1-7% is standard). Generally, these sales range in the hundreds of dollars offering the website owner a much larger pay per click than is typically received from display ads.

One of the largest companies to offer a large selection of affiliates is Commission Junction. This is a third party company that brings advertisers who want to use affiliate marketing together with website publishers who would like to provide their ad space to them. Their system keeps track of ad clicks and tracks sales. Commission Junction then receives payments from the advertisers and sends checks to the website publisher.

In addition, some companies take on the task of offering affiliate programs themselves, like Amazon, and offer this service directly to website owners allowing them to make widgets and banners to place on their own website.

Case Study

Business at Work

The ROCKVILLE BRIDGE™

For revenue, The Rockville Bridge relies on six possible sources of revenue. This includes one book, four products, and advertising revenue. Below is an overview of each revenue source and the companies chosen to supply the products or service.

Book

The book, titled "90 Days to Rockville," is sold through CreateSpace. The book is approximately 150 pages and printed in black and white. This keeps costs down and allows the book pricing to be reasonable. Using CreateSpace allows the book to be listed on Amazon, a brand many people are comfortable ordering from.

Products

In addition to the book, four different products are offered through Zazzle. These products include a T-shirt, coffee mug, apron, and postcard. So why this product mix? Well, since this location is a minor landmark, I could not find anyone else offering postcards showing this location. Visitors interested in this location or having taken a trip there, may be interested in a postcard from the location. The apron may be a bit more surprising; however, it is actually a useful product for model builders. When working, it is handy to keep tools close by and since the tools model makers use are small, an apron is a good way to hold them all in one place. The t-shirt and coffee mugs are much less useful but if someone is interested in the location, they may want to show it off by wearing a shirt or drinking out of a coffee mug with the logo.

The reason for using Zazzle on this business was that if offers a free customizable storefront to sell all of the items through. They also offer a fair royalty on the products.

Advertising

There are two sources of advertising revenue on the site – Google Adsense and Amazon Affiliates. Google Adsense serves display ads with relevant ads on pages within The Rockville Bridge website. There is also coding for Amazon affiliates which provides a commission whenever someone clicks from The Rockville Bridge site to Amazon and makes a purchase, including when they buy a copy of the "90 Days to Rockville" book.

CHAPTER 5

Marketing and Sales Plan

Chapter 5
Marketing and Sales Plan

The marketing and sales plan that you create for your business will be one of the single biggest factors to whether you succeed or you fail. As has been discussed, the on-demand business model bypasses the gatekeepers from keeping your content away from customers; however, it also means that you will not have the same marketing and sales support to make consumers aware that your product exists. This means the ball is completely in your court.

A marketing and sales plan should explain how every interaction with a potential customer is under taken. Even simple emails to respond to a question should be reflective of your marketing and sales plan. What a marketing and sales plan is not shouting "Buy my product!" at every person you meet. This may get you a few sales but probably turns away many potential customers as well. The marketing and sales plan is more involved. To keep the ideas simple, we will use the famous four P's of marketing to explain how to integrate your plan. These four P's of marketing are product, price, placement, and promotion.[3] By putting together an effective plan around these core areas,

---

[3] The four P's model was developed in the 1960s by Professor E. Jerome McCarthy at Michigan State University.

you will have a solid start to your marketing and sales efforts. As you become more sophisticated, you may want to refine the details in your plan. The Resources section at the end of the book offers some additional resources if you want to go deeper than this plan.

Product

The first part of the marketing plan is a thorough evaluation and decision about all the details of the product and services you are going to provide. In Chapter 5, you made your decisions about what products or service you were going to offer. Now is the time to decide the details about what you will offer.

Let's use an author who wants to publish a book as an example to illustrate the number of decisions that need to be made when designing a product. On the surface, a book may appear to be a fairly standard product but there are so many details that set one book apart from another. Here are just a few of the decisions that need to be made at this point for the author;

- ✓ Will the book be paperback or hardcover?
- ✓ Will it be printed in black and white or color?
- ✓ What fonts will it use?
- ✓ What will the cover look like (images, colors)?
- ✓ How many pages will it be?

- ✓ What type of paper?
- ✓ What will the size of the book be?
- ✓ What is the orientation of the book (landscape or portrait)?
- ✓ What will be the writing style (formal, conversational)?
- ✓ What will the page layout look like?
- ✓ Will the book include images?

Some of these decisions will be dictated by what you learned about your potential customer in your market research. These decisions about your product will carry through to what you will be able to charge and your promotions.

Price

The price that you charge for your products is important. There are several factors to consider before setting your price.

- ✓ What is the typical price range for the product you are selling?
- ✓ Who is your competition and what is their price?
- ✓ How much value are you adding to your customer?

Let's go back to the example of an author who wants to publish a book. The author has decided to write a non-fiction how to guide, printed in a typical trade paperback style. What is the typical price range for the product being sold? Consumer expectations for a non-fiction paperback book would be in the $10 to $50 range depending upon the content provided. It may be even higher for textbooks or technical manuals. What are the competitors typically selling their books for? A quick search through Amazon in the category shows narrows down price range from approximately $15 to $25 dollars. How much value is the author adding? Well, this is always the difficult part to determine. It appears as though the market for similar books would say that a book priced somewhere around $15 to $25 would match customer expectations. If the author wanted to price the book at $50, it may be difficult for a customer to make the choice to purchase that book compared to a competitors. However, if the author can somehow prove that the book buyer will receive that much additional value from their book, it may be a fair price.

Part of putting together an effective marketing and sales plan is finding the right price for the product offered. Take a hard look at the product you are offering and determine what a consumer would be willing to pay for it. If our example author wrote a 50 page manual and charged $100 for it, there would probably be a severe disconnect between the product and price. For this reason, ask yourself, does this price for this product make sense?

Placement

Placement refers to where consumers can purchase your product. This book is geared towards those only selling through one channel: the internet. However, for discussions in this book, the placement will refer to what sites you will be able to sell your products through.

As discussed in Chapter 4, all of the on-demand companies offer users the opportunity to set up their own store front through their company. If you are selling a book, CD, or DVD, some of the companies offer expanded distribution to other retailing websites like Amazon and Barnes and Noble. Why is this important? Well, those retailers have established themselves as reputable online retailers allowing many customers to feel comfortable purchasing products through those sites. Not everyone will be as familiar or comfortable using, for example, a Lulu storefront since it is not as established a brand as Amazon. There is a tradeoff in smaller royalties for selling through these main stream retail outlets but it may allow for more sales. What is important is to determine what the best channel for your product is. Make sure it makes the most sense and allows you to produce the product you want and sell it at the price that makes sense.

Promotions

This is what most people consider to be marketing their product. Promotions is simply how do you spread the word that your product exists and that it provides enough value to someone that they should purchase it.

When you decide on your promotional strategy, it should complement the products you have made, the price you are selling them at, and the placement you have chosen to sell them through. Using our author example again, the language that is used to describe the book on the back cover should be the same found in the book synopsis on the store page the item is being sold through. It should also be the same on the website for the book and the same in the promotional materials. If you have the option, the color schemes, fonts, logos, and images should all be consistent to reinforce the message being sent.

There are two types of promotions to consider: online and off-line. Online promotions focus on activities directly on the web. This is where you should spend most of your time as an internet business as the goal is to drive traffic to your site. Off-line promotions are important but don't always produce the immediate traffic that online activities can promote; however, offline activities can certainly reinforce what you are doing online.

Online Promotions

There are three main methods to promote your business online. These are social networking, paid advertisements, and link placement. There is a fourth, search engine optimization, but that will be discussed in Chapter 6 – Developing Your Web Presence.

Social Networking

One powerful way to create a lasting customer is to develop a presence on social networks. This means setting up a Facebook Fan Page or Group, a Twitter account, MySpace page, You Tube Channel or other relevant social network for your product. Once these are set up, the job has just begun. You need to use these tools to stay in touch with customers and continuously provide them with useful content.

Let's use the Facebook Fan Page as an example of actively using social networking to market your business. (We will discuss more about setting up social networks in Chapter 6 – Build Your Web Presence). The Fan Page allows you to send out communications to your fans through a status update.

These are generally short one or two sentence updates.

If you are selling a DVD, for example, don't update your status everyday by saying "Buy My DVD at Amazon."[4] This is a turnoff and does not add any value to your fans. Some will already have your DVD and this update will only clutter up their News Feed. If you have managed to attract a following to your Fan Page, the followers are most likely interested in the content of your DVD. Therefore, update your status with relevant information about your content. Maybe there is an interesting article you have found online that is relevant to what the DVD is about. This would be an ideal item to share. It adds some value to your fans because they might be interested in that too. This quickly reinforces what you are trying to sell.

The Fan Page also provides an opportunity for your followers to provide you with feedback. This can be both positive and negative so it is important to pay attention. Depending upon the settings that you chose when you set up your Fan Page, followers have the opportunity to post comments to your status updates,

---

[4] The exception is a new product announcement. You should let your followers know that you have something new available. However, this should not be your only communication to your followers and fans.

your wall, and even upload their own fan photos and videos.

Whichever social networking medium you decide works best for your business, it is important to come up with a plan and continue to be active with it. This is a continuous activity and it is important to reinforce what your products are. You don't need to post items every hour but come up with something to post once or twice and week to keep your business top of mind with your followers.

Paid Advertisements

An option you do have is to pay to advertise your business online. There are many different places to buy ads for the web and it is important to figure out where your customers are. For example, if you have a product that might capture the interest of a large group of people, it might be advantageous to use something like Google's Adwords to have your ad placed in search results and other websites with relative content. Microsoft and Yahoo both offer similar programs which place your ad in search results and on their own ad networks.

In addition, many niche websites also sell their own ad space. This can be tremendously beneficial if you have a product that would be of interest. The rates can vary compared to other web advertising options.

Link Placement

This is one of the broader categories and includes activities that get links to your site all over the web. One of the best ways to do this is to become active in the online communities where your products will have value. This means joining various discussion groups and message boards and actively discussing the relevant topics. This does not mean shamelessly promoting your product but instead providing constructive comments to the discussion. Most allow you to set up a profile and have a website link. Some of these discussion groups also have a link page so you can try to get yours published with the group.

In addition, you should spend time reading and commenting on blogs or articles related to your business. Again, this is not about shameless self promotion, but showing that you add some value to the conversation. If you know some prominent bloggers, online magazines, or news sites within your niche, you could approach them about reviewing your product or offer to be an interview subject. By appearing in one of these articles, you can gain some credibility and get some free advertising.

Off Line Promotions

While you should direct most of your efforts online, it would be unwise to forget about offline activities.

There are many simple activities that you can do to promote your business offline.

One of the easiest is to always carry business cards. You just never know when you are going to strike up a conversation with someone and find a person who might be interested in what you have done. These are relatively inexpensive and will be a valuable offline promotion.

Another inexpensive idea is to offer to take up speaking opportunities or provide demonstrations or clinics or perform depending upon what you content is. This will give you a chance to show off what you do best and make what you are doing more concrete in their minds. Plus, if you leave a good impression, people are always more comfortable purchasing something from a person they have met before than someone they have never heard of before.

Just like approaching a blogger or online magazine to review your products, you can do the same for other types of media. If you are legitimately an expert for something you have done, you might be able to be a guest on a local radio or television program to discuss what you know. If you have a book, CD, or DVD, you could also approach magazines or local newspapers to see if they would be interested in doing a review of the product. Sometimes they are hesitant to review a publish on-demand book but if your content is relevant to the readership of the publication, they might be willing to give it a chance and review it.

If you have the budget, there are many different paid advertising activities to promote your business. You can take out ads in magazines, newspapers, television or radio. You could also look into local sponsorship opportunities. Depending upon how successful you have been, these may want to wait until you've started to build some momentum with your business. Generally, these are fairly pricey and take time and lots of repetition to get results.

If you want to take the risk and purchase inventory of your products, you can also attend a trade show, flea market, festival, or other event to sell your products. This involves many additional expenses including renting your space, getting a sales tax license with the state where you are selling items, as well as making a display, brining money for change, and creating receipts. Attending events also doubles as a promotional effort so you will also want to print out some flyers or business cards for people to take with them if they don't want to purchase your product that day. This also has the side benefit of giving people who have already purchased your product an opportunity to meet you. In addition, it gives you a chance to say thank you and also solicit some feedback about what they liked and didn't like.

Case Study

Business at Work

The ROCKVILLE BRIDGE™

For The Rockville Bridge, the marketing mix is very straightforward.

Products

The products offered are a 150 page trade paperback book, a cotton T-Shirt, an apron, a postcard, and a coffee mug. All of the products have the company logo or feature a photo of the bridge.

Price

The book price was set at $19.95. This was to keep it in line with other paperback model railroad books. For the other products the prices were set at $22.95 for shirts, $19.95 for the apron, $0.95 for postcards, and $14.95 for the coffee mug.

Placement

Obviously, all of the products are sold online. There are three channels that a consumer can purchase products through – two for the book and one for the other merchandise. The book was published through CreateSpace. This allows the book to be listed on Amazon as well as have its own store page on CreateSpace. The other products sold through a storefront on Zazzle. This store front was the only one that was customizable. The same header from the website was added to the store and the color scheme was changed to match the website.

Promotion

A number of inexpensive online and offline promotions were used. There was no paid advertising due to this being such a small market. Online promotions included setting up social networking accounts such as a Facebook Fan Page, Twitter Account, and a YouTube Channel. The social networks were used to stay in contact with followers of the site and a plan for weekly updates was put in place.

In addition, there are numerous websites devoted to links for model railroad hobbyist so the site was listed with as many of them as possible. In addition, limited activity was taken up on relevant message boards and communities.

Offline activities included sending the book to several model railroad magazines to be reviewed. It was picked up by one and was the lead book in their monthly reviews. In addition, a copy of the book was sent to the Bridgeview Bed and Breakfast, which overlooks the bridge with a poster of the book for the owner to hang for guests to see. The owner was kind enough to do so. (It helps to feature them in the book!)

CHAPTER 6

Create Your Products

Chapter 6
Create Your Products

At this point, it is finally time to actually produce your products. This is your time to shine. This is where you need to do what you do best and create the finest quality products that will add value to your customers. Obviously, you should know what you need to do to make the best content but there are some technical items to keep in mind for your end results.

The rest of the chapter is an overview of the typical technical requirements for each type of product and some methods to make them. This is by no means all inclusive but if you are unfamiliar with how to make these products, it will give you a head start. All of the on-demand companies list their technical requirements for each of their products on their website. Don't be afraid to investigate the requirements for each as well as to ask questions on the community forums provided on each site for more in-depth help.

Books

Creating a book that is ready for press is not a very technical process, but it does require some planning and the proper software. All the companies that print books on-demand require a press-ready PDF for the interior of the book as well as one for the cover of the book.

The interior pages of the book can be written in any word processing program that you can think of as long as the pages can eventually be converted to a PDF. When you begin to write your book you will want to setup the pages for your book. Check with the company that you want to use to determine what size book you can create. Start by setting this as your page size. Then set your margins. These are usually a bit of personal preference but you will have to follow the minimum inside margin requirement so that all the text you write can be read. Also remember that your interior book file has to have an even number of pages. Generally, each chapter should start on the odd number pages but again, this is personal preference. The content of the book is completely up to you. You can pick your fonts, colors, images, graphics, and anything else you can think of.

After you are done writing and formatting your book, it is time to prepare the PDF file. Make sure that the final output is at least 300 dpi. If you have Adobe Acrobat Pro, you can change the settings in the dialog box that opens when you go to convert your document to a PDF. Make sure that all your fonts are embedded in the file.

When it comes to designing a cover for your book, there are a couple of options. Most of the book publishers have free cover creator programs built into their system. This is very helpful if you do not have the artistic skills to design a cover yourself or have access to the software to design a cover. If you do have the software and the artistic touch, all of the companies offer templates to download which allow you to create your own cover.

eBooks

If you want to publish your book as an eBook, there are some differences from a physical book. Generally, there are two options for creating your eBook. The first method is to just use your original PDF book interior file. This is an option with a service like Lulu. However, many eBook reading devices are better suited to use the ePub language, an open-source digital standard for coding of your book. The standards are handled by the International Digital Publishing Forum (IDPF). The standard consists of XHTML for the book content, XML for descriptions, and a zip file in which everything is placed. If you have the background with programming languages, these books are not difficult to make. In addition, this source allows for the addition of Digital Rights Management (DRM) to be attached to the book. As the publisher and author, you will have the option to offer this level of security on your book if you are worried about people making illegal copies of your book.

CDs

Generally, print on-demand CDs are associated with audio CDs, but some companies, like Lulu, also offer data CDs if you want to sell a software program, data sets, or any other sets of files that would fit onto the CD. Generally, the requirements for each type of CD are a bit different.

If you are creating an audio CD, you will have to produce your audio tracks in MP3, AIFF, or WAV format. Whatever mixing program you are using for your final output will need to be able to create tracks in this format. Generally, you have the option to directly upload these final files into the companies system or mail them a final CD with your tracks on them. All track title information is added when you set up the project on the company's website.

If you are creating a data CD, it is just a matter of uploading the data to the companies system or sending them a final disc with everything you want on it included.

You will also need to create artwork for your CD. Each company provides templates for the artwork for both the CD and the case that it comes in. Usually these files are an image format, such as a .jpg, .png, or a number of other formats. For more information about programs to use to create this artwork, see the Graphics and Artwork section.

DVD

Just like the CD, print on-demand DVDs are associated with video, but some companies, again Lulu, also offer data DVDs if you want to sell a software program, data sets, or any other sets of files that would fit onto the DVD. Generally, the requirements for each type of DVD are a bit different.

If you are creating a video DVD, you will have to produce your video with a single VIDEO_TS and AUDIO_TS file format. Whatever video editing program you are using for your final output will need to be able to create tracks in this format. Generally, you have the option to directly upload these final files into the company's system or mail them a final DVD with your tracks on them.

If you are creating a data DVD, it is just a matter of uploading the data to the company's system or sending them a final disc with everything you want on it included.

You will also need to create artwork for your DVD. Each company provides templates for the artwork for both the disc and the case that it comes in. Usually these files are an image format, such as a .jpg, .png, or a number of other formats. For more information about programs to use to create this artwork, see the Graphics and Artwork section below.

Graphics and Artwork

One of the common elements of all the print on-demand products is the need for graphics. Producing graphics and artwork can be a bit of a whirlwind if you have never attempted to do so before. There is an alphabet soup of file extensions and printing types. There are things called resolution and DPI. What to make of it all? Let's break down all the pieces and how to create great graphics that print well.

Let's start with understanding resolution and dots per inch (DPI). These terms may seem like they are the same but they are not. Resolution is simply the size of your photo measured in the unit of pixels. For example, a square photo whose height and width is 1000 pixels each, would be considered a 1 megapixel photo (or a 1000x1000 pixel photo.) DPI is used to print your image. Let's say you take that 1000x1000 pixel photo and wanted to place it on a 10"x10" object, you would need to print it at 100 DPI. For every inch, you would have 100 pixels. If you only wanted a 1"x1" image, you would print the same photo at 1000 DPI. Generally speaking, almost all printers are setup to run at 300 DPI, so whatever size image you want to print, you need to convert this to come up with the resolution of the artwork you need to create. Take the cover on this book. It is 6"x9" and printed at 300 DPI. Therefore, the resolution of the file created for the cover is 1800x2700 pixels.

Once you understand what resolution and printing size you need, the next step is to determine the best image file type to use. There are a number of options and not all are accepted by each on-demand printer so take a look at the one you want to use before creating your image. Some of the image file types are:

- ✓ .JPG-The .jpg is the most well known image file format and will support over 16 million colors. However, the purpose of the .jpg file is to compress the image. There are subtle changes to colors and lines which might make the image appear more blurry than another file format.
- ✓ .BMP-This is the Microsoft Windows Bitmap format and it saves your file pixel for pixel. This is a nice feature but is not supported by many of the print on-demand companies and is generally a very large file size.

- PNG–This format is a completely loss-less compression. Gradients come out much smoother and do not have the distortions that may appear in a .jpg.
- .PSD-This is the PhotoShop Document image file and is arguably the best quality file format. It keeps all the information about the photo in an uncompressed format so file sizes will be very large.
- .TIFF-Tag Image File image format is similar to a .psd file in that it keeps all the original information about the image but the layers are flattened. This again keeps the file sizes large compared to other formats.

If you want to create your own artwork, each of the print on-demand companies offers templates for all of their graphic requirements. You can then use these in your favorite image editing software. At the very high-end, is Adobe Photoshop. If you plan on making a lot of graphics this is worth the expense. There are also free programs such as Google's Picasa program which offers limited photo editing and some PC programs like Microsoft Office Picture Manager and Paint programs. These basic programs will produce reasonable graphics.

Case Study

Business at Work

The ROCKVILLE BRIDGE™

So how was all the content created for The Rockville Bridge? There was a number of different software programs used, mostly programs already included on almost anyone's home computer.

Book Interior

The book, "90 Days to Rockville," was written in Microsoft Word. All the images in the book were converted to black and white before inserting them in the document in Google's Picasa program. This program is offered as a free download. The one piece of software that wasn't included on the computer when I purchased it and bought separately was Adobe Acrobat Pro. This was used to convert the document to a final PDF. If you do not want to purchase this product, Adobe does provide a free trial version online to convert documents to PDF. This doesn't have all the functions but does work if you can't afford the software.

Book Cover

To make the cover, CreateSpace offers an online Cover Creator program. They have several templates available. To customize the template, several images are required. Fortunately, I had taken several photos that didn't require any cosmetic editing before placing them into the Cover Creator template. However, two of the images needed to be resized so that they fit within the dimensions of the template. Finally, all the product descriptions and text were added.

Product Logos

Would you believe it if I told you that The Rockville Bridge logo, the one you see at the start of each of these "Business at Work" sections was made in Microsoft Word? I hope so because that is what I used. It turned out to be a fairly simple process. One of the nice features of Adobe Acrobat Pro is that you can convert a PDF to several different image files. Once the logo was created in Word, I saved the document as a PDF and then exported the image file I needed.

This has proven to be a very quick way to modify the logo design to suit the many different color needs for the products. For example, the logo in this book is black with a gray background. On the website, it is in gold with a maroon background. On the t-shirt products available on the Zazzle store, it needed a transparent background with the gold lettering and logo. Each of these logos was a different size which was easy to edit with the included Microsoft Office Picture Manager software on my PC.

CHAPTER 7

Build Your Web Presence

Chapter 7
Build Your Web Presence

You are almost ready to go! You have a business plan, researched your market, picked your products, shaped a marketing and sales plan, and created your products. The final piece of the puzzle is to build your web presence. This will include building your website, setting up social networking sites, blogs, formatting your graphics, and optimizing everything for the web.

Website

Since you are setting up an internet business, you need to have a home base online. This is your website. From here, you should have links to your products, social networking sites, blogs, and content of interest.

At a very basic level, all websites need a domain and webhosting. The domain is your web address and webhosting is where the files for your website are stored so anyone can view them. There are numerous companies that you can purchase a domain name and webhosting through. Just remember, you are in effect leasing both of these items for a period of time. For example, the domain www.businessinminutes.com was initially purchased for one year. This will need to be renewed every year that the website is active. Same is true for webhosting. You lease space for a period of time. Generally, the increments are one year in length but some providers offer shorter or longer services.

While you are purchasing your domain name and webhosting service, you might also want to consider purchasing an email hosting account. This will allow you to have an email address that will have your domain in your email. For example, if you want to send an email to me, use jim@businessinminutes.com. This goes back to your marketing plan. It will look more professional to have your domain instead of yourname@yahoo.com as your email address.

Once you have the domain you want and hosting lined up, it is time to build your website. Depending upon your knowledge of building websites, you will have to make some decisions about how to proceed. If you have lots of knowledge and experience building websites, just head off to the races and skip the rest of this section. If the idea of building a website has you shaking in your shoes, follow along for some options.

There are basically three paths to take if you have no experience in building a website. First, you can grab any how to build a basic website book and dive in. You will be surprised by just how easy it is to build a very simple site. Second, when purchasing web site hosting, some of these companies, such as GoDaddy.com, offer packages that have prebuilt website templates to build your own site that do not require you to touch any code. They all have graphic user interfaces so just input your information and what you see is what you get. This can be a bit limiting but an option. The third option is to pay someone else to build your site. This is the most expensive option.

If you decide to go ahead and build your site, expect a bit of a learning curve but it will serve you well. There are software programs out there such as Microsoft Expressions and Adobe Dreamweaver that can help beginners build a website easily. These offer the ability to edit the code as well as edit the page graphically. This will help you learn how the code you are writing is showing up in the finished product. You can build some very slick websites with these programs that can serve you very well as you launch your business.

Taking the time to learn how to build your own site will serve you well for a number of reasons. If you understand the basics of coding, you will discover how many of the social networking websites described in the next section can be even more customized with the knowledge of a little HTML programming. In addition, if your business grows and you want to hire someone to build a more technically complicated site, you will be able to have more meaningful conversations with potential website programmers than if you didn't know the difference between Java and coffee.

Social Media

The next important part of your web presence to setup is all the social networking sites you plan to use. These are increasingly becoming a central core of any marketing strategy. There is no need to be on every social networking site. Just pick the ones that are most relevant to what audience you are trying to reach and you feel most comfortable using on a regular basis.

To give you an idea of just the sheer number of different options, here is a list of just 15 different sites, some general and some niche focused, that you could use for your business:

- ✓ Facebook – General interest
- ✓ Twitter – General interest
- ✓ MySpace – General interest
- ✓ Bebo – General interest
- ✓ LinkedIn – Business networking
- ✓ YouTube – Video Sharing
- ✓ Flickr – Photo Sharing
- ✓ Picasa – Photo Sharing

- ✓ DeviantArt - Art
- ✓ quarterlife – Art/Music
- ✓ iLike - Music
- ✓ Digital Rodeo - Music
- ✓ Reverb Nation - Music
- ✓ LibraryThing - Books
- ✓ aNobii - Books

Again, you don't need to have a presence on all of them; just the ones that are right for your audience and you feel comfortable with. There are literally hundreds of different social networks from general interest to niche focus.

Once you have chosen the social networks you want to use, you will need to customize them to reflect your business. Each is a bit different but most of them have you upload a profile photo and profile information such as a website and About sections. In addition, many of the sites allow you to change the color scheme or add background image. Take advantage of this feature to add continuity between the graphic design of your website and other social networking sites.

After you have taken the time to setup your social networking sites, don't forget to add the links, widgets, and badges to your main website. Almost all social networking sites have tools which automatically generate these and usually can be customized to match the graphics of your website. You can also add the Share This Buttons to each page of your site to easily allow visitors to spread the word about the great new business they have just found.

Blogging

In addition to social networking sites, another option is to start a blog for your venture. The advantage of a blog verses just using a social networking site is that you can provide more information in longer updates than you can, say, by updating your Twitter feed with 140 characters.

There are several options for blogging. You can add the tools to your own hosted website or you can use already hosted sites such as Google's Blogger or Wordpress. Both are good choices for creating news updates or providing relevant articles for what you are trying to communicate.

If you feel like investing in some equipment beyond your computer, you could also try your hand at video blogging or even podcasting (audio blogging) if you'd rather not write. There are plenty of people who would rather watch a video or listen to a podcast in their car on a commute than read a 1000 word blog post. This will require either a video camera for video blogging or a microphone and audio editing software for a podcast. Fortunately, there are inexpensive options for both. If you want to create a video blog, there are plenty of video cameras or digital cameras with video functionality available for under $200. These usually come with all the software you need to get the videos from your camera to your computer. Most of the video editing options are limited but you can just upload your videos directly onto YouTube or a social networking site of choice. If a podcast is of more interest to you, a basic microphone and free audio editing software, such as Audacity, will allow you to make audio recordings very quickly. These can just be uploaded to your website for users to download.

Graphic Design

One of the keys to all pieces of your web presence and products is flawless graphic design. While the old adage, "Don't judge a book by its cover" may be great life lesson but that is just not how people respond to products. The graphic design used on your sites can make or break the product you are trying to sell. This includes everything from logos to color schemes to fonts. With that said there is no right or wrong to graphic design but rather understanding who is going to purchase your products and what they are expecting.

Let's think through an example. Let's say you are building a sports business geared towards adult men.

Should your logo have flowers, be printed in pink, and have a calligraphy font? I'm going to guess no. A better choice would be colors that would resonate with that group such as blues, grays, or maybe blacks. This is the art of graphic design.

The second part of graphic design is to have consistency between your products and websites. If you have a logo, it should be on everything. If you have a specific font that you want to work with, have that everywhere. Is the color scheme that you have chosen the same? If you have images, are they the same everywhere? This consistency will allow users to feel more comfortable with your brand as well as make you appear more professional since you have your act together enough to make everything be consistent.

Search Engine Optimization

While technically a marketing operation, the time for implementing Search Engine Optimization (SEO) is as you build your website and web presence. SEO is basically building your site in such a way as to organically reach as high as possible in search engine rankings. As mentioned in Chapter 5, there are two ways to reach the top of the search engine rankings. The easiest is to pay for advertising. The second is to use the right keywords on your site to be at the top of the list when users search.

While all search engines are a bit different, there are three ways that search results are arrived at when someone clicks on the search button. They are:

- ✓ Relevant keywords
- ✓ Number of external links to the site
- ✓ How recently the site was updated

There are entire companies and consulting firms devoted to SEO so there are a multitude of ideas that can be implemented. However, at a very basic level, you will need to address those three issues to move your site higher in the rankings.

Keywords are the most important search criteria. Let's say you were interested in finding business books. You would go to your favorite search engine and type in business books. The highest search results will have the keywords business books somewhere on their site. Generally, the search engines look at the page title and the text within in headings and the body to find these keywords. Take a look at the Business in Minutes website and you will see numerous keywords that described the book and the blog as well as in the page title across the top of the browser. These are very simple additions to your site. If you know some of the key terms that people will be searching, add those to the text on your site as well as the page title.

Even if you have all the right keywords on your site, if no one has placed a link to your site, you will move down in the rankings. The idea is that your site has not been proven interesting enough for other people to want to share. Therefore it is important to generate some buzz for your site and make sure there are people sharing the link and placing it all over the web.

One of the final pieces that the search engine will look at is how long has it been since you updated your site. It is amazing, but a search engine such as Google will crawl[5] your site on a very regular basis. The more changes you make, the more regularly it will look. The idea is that the more dynamic the site, the more relevant and up to date the content will be.

If you are successful in implementing this strategy and operating in a niche market, you will be amazed at how high you can reach. You might even find yourself in the number one spot!

---

[5] A fancy term for saying that they look at your site

Case Study

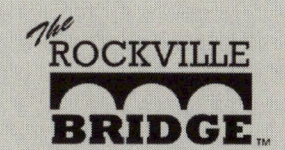

Business at Work

The Rockville Bridge has several portals on the web including the main website as well as several social networking sites.

Website

The main website, www.therockvillebridge.com, was designed and built using Microsoft Expressions using XHTML and CSS. There are only a total of 10 pages to the website but it provides relevant information about the real bridge, the model of the bridge, visitors guide, and information about the book. The home page on the site has links to all of the social networking sites as well as to the store.

Social Media

Due to the part-time nature of the business, a total of four social networking sites were chosen: Facebook, Twitter, YouTube, and Picasa. These were sites that I knew I could update with limited amounts of time and had large enough audiences that there were probably people in my target audience who were using those sites. Each site was customized to include the logo, the chosen color scheme, and an image of the bridge that was used on the book cover.

Graphic Design

The graphic design for the websites was fairly straight forward. After the logo design, the main choice was the use of a maroon and gold color throughout the products. Why? Since the market research told us that the group of potential customers were railroad enthusiasts who were in interested in the Pennsylvania Railroad, a subtle reminder in color choice was made. The maroon and gold colors are the same colors the Pennsylvania Railroad used. This would offer immediate familiarity to railroad enthusiast and would set the tone for a business about a Pennsylvania based landmark.

SEO

In order to make sure the website reached the top of the search engine rankings, the keyword Rockville Bridge was placed in the page titles on the websites as well as in the descriptions on the home page. As mentioned in Chapter 5, links were placed in as many places as possible to drive traffic to the site. Finally, about halfway through the year, a news feed was added to the home page to make sure the site could be updated regularly. Over the course of the year, these all paid off as the website moved into the number one search position on Google for the keyword 'Rockville Bridge.' Even the Facebook Fan Page eventually made the first page of results.

CHAPTER 8

Evaluate Your Results

Chapter 8
Evaluate Your Results

Congratulations! At this point you should be off to the races with your business. However, the fun has only just begun. Once you are up and running you have to keep tabs on your business to keep track of the results so you can make changes as necessary.

For this, it will be important to look at the numbers coming from your business. This will include the obvious such as sales but also web traffic and customer feedback. For this, you will need to set an accounting system and web analytics as well as a feedback system and a quick way to measure it all.

Accounting System

You will need to keep track of all your revenues and expenses in an accounting system. If you have a very simple business, you may be able to keep track of everything in a spreadsheet program. If you have a number of products with different suppliers, you might want a more advanced accounting system, such as QuickBooks from Intuit. This is not necessary if you are at a small scale but any type of accounting software will offer powerful analytic reports that can quickly summarize all of your transactions. This will save you some time and allow you to make decisions about strategy much faster than if you had to put everything together yourself.

Web Analytics

Another important piece of data that is important to keep an eye on is the traffic to your websites. This is much more in depth than just a simple visitor counter on your website. Today, there are sophisticated, and free, web tools available that will track everything about the visitors to your site. They will not only tell you how many visitors dropped by but it will also tell you how long they stayed, if they came back, how many pages they visited when they stopped by, how they got there, what search terms they found you with, and more.

This is a treasure trove of data that can help analyze how you are doing and allow you to make changes to see improvement. For example, are the majority of your websites visitors going to see just one portion of your site and ignoring another part? This could show what visitors are mostly interested in or point out that you have incorrectly named a section of your site. Also, how long are the visitors hanging around for? Are they only stopping by for ten seconds and then click away to the next stop on the web. That could indicate poor graphic design or a lack of valuable information to keep them around.

Generally, these web analytics can be set up through your hosting company or through a paid analytics company. If you want a free service, try Google Analytics. It is free and all you will need to do is set up an account and place a small snippet of code into each page that you would like to track. Within a few days, you will be able to see lots of information about your traffic and download that to your favorite spreadsheet program for analysis.

Another part of the web analytics is to track your fans and followers on your social networks. Some of these services offer web analytics services for free (such as Facebook) that will give you basic demographic information about your fans as well as the traffic to your page. This data is important to confirm your market research and see if you need to make any changes to your marketing efforts.

Determine Metrics

Once you have all of these raw data sources, it is time to determine which metrics you will use to analyze your business and see if you are on track. Some of these are straightforward while others are more useful when you have been in business for a period of time and looking for growth strategies. Whichever metrics you decide to use, make sure that you regularly plan to spend some time gathering the data and analyzing everything. To that end, some of the metrics that you will want to keep track of are as follows:

- ✓ Sales

This will be the easiest to keep track of and most important. If you aren't making any money, you won't be in business for very long! However, you will want to track sales to see if you have a season item or have items that sell well on weekdays compared to weekends. This will give you a better idea of when to focus your marketing efforts as well. For example, if you are using paid advertising and your items only sell at graduation time for high school seniors, there is no point in advertising in August.

- ✓ Sales per visitor/fan/follower

In addition to just tracking sales, you will want to look at sales metrics against the traffic that you have coming to your site. This will be important as your business grows and develops. If you have a mix of t-shirts, books, and DVDs, for example, you might want to know which items sell better based upon the traffic to your site. You might discover that the total number of DVDs sold per visitor is small compared to the number of t-shirts you are selling, but you earn more dollars per visitor with the DVD. This might make you think about producing another DVD instead of another t-shirt as you will earn more money even if you might sell a smaller quantity.

- ✓ Ad revenue per visitor

If you decide to add advertising as a revenue stream on your website, you will want to keep track of the amount of revenue you earn based on the number of ad clicks as well as the total traffic across your site.

- ✓ Customer acquisition cost

If you are using paid advertising, you will want to determine what your customer acquisition cost is. This is a simple equation. Take the total advertising dollars spent and divide that by the total number of items sold. This will be your customer acquisition cost. If you spent $50 on advertising and sold 10 items, your customer acquisition cost will be $5. This number will give you a sense of how effective your marketing has been.

- ✓ Wage per hour

One of the items that are generally ignored in a part time business analysis is how much are you actually making per hour. Is this business really worth the time you are putting in? For this, you will need to keep track of your time as well as the net income of your business. To determine the wage per hour take the net income and divide that by the number of hours worked. If you are not making a wage you feel comfortable with, you should take some time and reassess whether you want to continue with the business or how effective you are being with your time.

Customer Feedback

Despite all the best intentions of studying the market and testing a product, you will never get complete feedback until you begin to actually selling a product. One of the important metrics to determine how you are doing is the feedback you receive from customers.

You will need to make sure to have plenty of places and opportunities to allow your customers to get in touch with you to tell you how you are doing. It is nice to hear how well you are doing, but it is more important to listen to any negative feedback you are receiving. This could alert you to potential flaws or problems with your products. It also may alert you to a potential market or idea that you are missing.

Case Study

Business at Work

The ROCKVILLE BRIDGE™

So did the business succeed financially? Well, let's break down the numbers:

Revenues	Units	Totals
Books	152	$1437
T-shirts	12	28
Postcards	40	4
Aprons	17	34
Coffee mugs	0	0
Google advertising	1	86
Amazon Affiliates	1	42
Total revenue		**$1631**
Expenses		
Domain Name		$10
Website Hosting		75
Printed Flyers		20
Postage		30
Proof Books		22
Total Expenses		**$157**
Net Income		**$1474**

As you can see, the site was profitable for the first year. However, this does not take into account the time it took for the site to be built or the time spent working on it once it was up and running. So to be complete, let's see how the site fairs when that is taken into account.

As mentioned in Chapter 2, the total time it took to write the book, make the products, and build the website was approximately 40 hours. In addition, once the site was up and running, about one to two hours a week was spent maintaining and marketing the business. For round numbers, let's call this another 50 hours invested. That means for the entire project, the total cost was 90 hours of my time. Now let's look and see what the return was on the business.

Net Income/Hours Worked = Wage per Hour

$1474/90 hours = $16.37/hour

That sure beats minimum wage but is certainly not making me rich. Since this was a micro market, this is a reasonable return. No one could quit their day job but the net income is not bad when you consider that it could pay for about a month of rent (depending upon where you live), a car payment or three, or a number of other living expenses. This also proves the point that you need to find a market that is large enough to support your desired financial returns. If you want to quit your job, you'd need to make a lot more than $1474 a year!

CHAPTER 9

Growing Your Business

Chapter 9
Growing Your Business

Now that you have built your business and are making money, the next step is to ask yourself, what's next? Everyone has a different answer to this question and much of your answer will be based on your market, your goals and ambition. For now, let's look at several different strategies to keep you motivated and growing your business to the next level.

Set Financial Goals

When you start your business, you should have some financial goals in mind, but after some time operating, you will have a better understanding about what is realistic and what you can expect to get out of it.

Here are just a few sample financial goals that you may set for yourself:

- ✓ Increase overall sales
- ✓ Increase sales of a particular product
- ✓ Decrease (or increase) advertising expenses
- ✓ Decrease customer acquisition cost
- ✓ Increase advertising revenue

You should be able to understand what it takes to reach each of these goals. Start by modify your sales and marketing plan to accommodate these new goals. This will help give you a concrete step by step guide of what actions you need to take every day to achieve your new financial goals.

Create New Products

One of the quick ways to capitalize upon your existing customer base is to introduce new on-demand products. These should be complimentary to your existing products and be relevant to your existing customer base.

One of the easiest ways to start is to ask yourself, can you make what you have done into a series? For example, if you have written a book, are there other relevant books that you can write to create a series. This will also serve as a marketing platform for all the books you have written as you get deeper into a series. Let's say a customer only discovers your books because the third one you wrote was a subject near and dear to them. If they like the one they read, they may go back and purchase the other two. This effect will take some time to see but can add to your bottom line in the future.

In addition, if you authored a book, is there a video, documentary, or movie that you could produce from your book? Similarly, if you made a documentary, is there a companion book that you could produce?

Again, this is another complimentary product that if someone buys one and likes it, they may be more interested in purchasing the other.

What if you are an artist that is selling photos or art prints on-demand? How about a photo book of your best sellers or a slideshow or a screensaver? Maybe you have a really cool photography process that might be of interest to serious photographers. You could create a how-to video to explain the process to others.

There are endless ideas that you can probably come up with for your business. Take some time to go back to your initial market research to determine what will make the best product choice.

Off Line Revenue

If you are fortunate enough to build a successful on-demand business, you might begin to consider ways to expand your revenue sources off line. This will mean more risk to your business as you invest in new projects, but you might find some highly profitable ventures.

There are plenty of ways to take what you do online and take advantage of it offline. For example, if you are an author and publish non-fiction books, you might be able to get access to paid speaking engagements at conferences. You might also be able to parlay that knowledge into consulting jobs.

Maybe you've made a movie. Hopefully, you've been able to figure out some other on-demand products to sell to merchandise your movie, but you could also have screenings of your movies that you sell tickets to. You probably won't get into a large chain movie theater but there may be options to rent out a local independent theater or hall for an evening.

Maybe your content would lend itself well to the sale of another unique product not available on-demand. Maybe you have a new exercise trend that requires new exercise equipment. Along with your on-demand workout DVD, you could also develop and sell the products needed for your exercise routine. Again, this requires a much larger investment of money and time, but allows you to expand your business to something with a better barrier to entry than just selling the workout DVD.

If you begin to explore making money offline, you will have to keep in mind some of the legal implications. If you have not incorporated, you should consider doing so before moving offline. In addition, if you plan on making actual sales, you will have to collect sales tax.[6]

---

[6] Remember, your on-demand products provide you a royalty payment. This is considered a different form of revenue for

For this, you will need to register for a sales tax number with your state.

Exit Strategy

What is your end goal? Every good business owner understands how they plan on exiting from the company they are starting. Many entrepreneurs dream of starting a business and imagining themselves ringing the opening bell at the New York Stock Exchange on the day of their company's initial public offering and cashing out their investment to the tune of millions of dollars. You can dream this dream if you want but ultimately, this will be an unrealistic expectation for your on-demand business. However, there are other successful exits.

If your product that you are producing has been very successful using the on-demand model, it may mean there is enough interest in your product that retailers may be interested in putting it in their stores. This will require gaining approval from the gatekeepers that this model helps you get around. However, these gatekeepers do still control access to many of the larger retail channels and can help take your product to the next level. If you have reached this point,

---

tax purposes than if you make a sale of a product yourself. Your on-demand service provider is required to collect sales tax, not you.

congratulations are in order. The big question to ask yourself will be whether or not you need their help if you can succeed on your own.

Another exit option if you build your brand correctly, will someone be interested in buying it? Many businesses are started with the idea that they can be built and eventually sold as a method to cash out on the initial investment. This is going to be a very difficult option, especially if you want to make a lot of money. As mentioned in Chapter 2, there are almost no barriers to entry for a competitor to enter the market. This means the only items you will be able to offer of value is your domain name, brand, trademarks, and content. Chances are you will have no other real assets that aren't simply commodities. This means the assets of value are all intangible and difficult to put a dollar figure on.

If you do find a buyer for your business, you will have to be realistic about what you can get for the business. Generally, businesses are bought and sold for a multiple of revenue or net income. For a small internet business this multiple will be small and vary depending upon your prospects for growth. However, if you have built a part time business from nothing to say $10,000 in two to three years, that would be a success!

Case Study

Business at Work

The ROCKVILLE BRIDGE™

With a year under its belt, The Rockville Bridge business will need to find new customers or add some new products to make the same amount of revenue in its second year.

Financial Goals

The first goal for The Rockville Bridge in its second year of operation will be to reach the $2000 level in sales. This is ambitious, to say the least, based on the market size but not impossible. There is the possibility of adding additional products to the mix which can add to the bottom line. In addition, there will probably be more traffic to the website as there is expansion plans to add some more content and articles which should be of interest to the site's existing user base.

New Products

There are several ideas for on-demand products to be added to the product line which can help add to the bottom line. Currently, the Zazzle store only has a small number of products available compared to what could be offered. For this reason, several more products such as a calendar, mouse pad, embroidered polo shirts, and bags are in the works. While the sales numbers for products were small, adding several additional items to the mix could help the bottom line. In addition, there is the possibility of adding another book about the history of the bridge along with a DVD of video from the bridge.

Off Line Revenue

One of the questions I am often asked is do I sell kits of the bridge? This has certainly got me thinking about offering an actual product of a scale model kit of the bridge. However, there is no on-demand kit making companies yet. So this strategy would require an investment in product development, kit production, and inventory. While I wouldn't take this idea off the table yet, this is probably too big a risk for the time I am putting into the business. The idea is certainly appealing and would allow me to build upon the customer base established with the book.

Exit Strategy

Admittedly, there is very little chance for a sale of this brand and business to fund my retirement. Most likely, another hobbyist with an interest in the bridge may want what I have built and continue to build upon it. As a part time business, the realistic exit strategy will be to close the doors when sales can no longer cover the costs to operate the business.

CHAPTER 10

Are you ready?

Chapter 10
Are you ready?

I hope the answer is yes. Now is the time. The only person that can make this happen is you. You have to put in the effort and stay disciplined. It will take time but with a solid plan, success can be yours.

Make the Choice

One of the biggest hurdles that face would be entrepreneurs and those building a business are simply deciding to make it happen. Everyone can daydream and think up great ideas, but you are the only one that can take that great idea and make it into a reality.

I'm sure you've had friends or acquaintances that always discuss their great idea or are always talking about a book they want to write. How many of those people ever follow through? Unless you are lucky enough to be surrounded by an incredibly motivated group of people, chances are the numbers of those people who follow through are small. Most people come up with plenty of excuses about what is stopping them from realizing their goals. It's the easier path. Don't be one of those people.

One of the great parts about building a business like the one described in this book is that the financial risk can be very small. The biggest risk will be the amount of time you spend building your business. Ask yourself is their some other activity that you can take out of your life, that you can replace with building a part time business? Do you really need to watch that TV show? Do you really need to spend five hours a day aimlessly surfing the web? When you are finally ready to say no, make the choice and decide to build your business.

Set Concrete Goals

Once you have made the choice to build a business, the next step is to set concrete milestones and goals. This is important so you can match your plan to day to day activities that you need to get done.

Let's use the example of weight loss and compare it to your business. Plenty of people every January have a New Year's Resolution to lose a certain number of pounds. That's an admiral goal but does not explain how to lose weight. A concrete goal would be to run two miles three days a week. That is an activity that can be accomplished with the net results typically being weight loss. For your business, you should do the same. You may have a goal of increasing sales to a certain level. Again, that is nice, but not concrete. What would be better is to tell yourself to spend an additional two hours a week contacting potential customers. This should translate into an increase in sales over time.

Do Not Be Afraid to Fail

In many ways, entrepreneurship is a lot like baseball. Think about the best baseball players of all time. If they are a hitter, what is their success rate of getting a hit when they go up to bat? At best it is only a one out of three chance. That means that two thirds of the time even the best baseball player goes to the plate, they fail. Think about that.

If you look at the greatest innovators, inventors, or entrepreneurs, you will quickly see that none of them have ever been perfect. They have all failed at some point. What is important is to recognize when it is over, understand what mistakes were made, and most importantly, get up and try it all over again.

I'm very confident that if you put in the effort, the time, and create a plan, you will be able to build a successful business. When you do, we'd love to hear about it. Contact us through our website at: www.businiessinmutes.com so we can share your success story.

Now get to work!

Business In Minutes
Resources

- ✓ Quick Start Checklist
- ✓ Example Business Plan
- ✓ Additional Reading
- ✓ On-Demand Websites

Resources
Quick Start Checklist

- ☑ Determine the business model
    - o Select revenue sources
    - o Evaluate costs
    - o Figure out total initial investment
- ☑ Research the market
    - o Who is the customer?
    - o How many potential customers are there?
    - o How does the customer shop?
    - o How easy is it to reach the potential customers?
    - o What value will the customers receive from the product?
- ☑ Pick the on-demand providers
    - o Books, CDs, DVDs, Products
- ☑ Develop sales and marketing plan
    - o What are the product, price, placement, and promotion?
- ☑ Create the products
- ☑ Build the web presence
    - o Website
    - o Social networks
    - o Blogs
    - o Graphic Design
    - o SEO
- ☑ Evaluate the results

Resources
Example Business Plan

The following section contains the actual business plan written for the sample company, The Rockville Bridge, featured in the *Business at Work* sections at the end of each chapter. Your business plan may be longer or have additional sections depending upon your business idea.

Executive Summary

The Rockville Bridge business will serve the model railroad and railroad enthusiast community who is interested in the world's longest stone masonry arch bridge – Rockville Bridge – located in Harrisburg, PA. The business will offer a how-to book about building a model of the bridge along with merchandise featuring the bridge and company logo. All of the activity of the business will be run through the website portal for the enterprise at www.therockvillebridge.com which will feature content about the bridge and models of it. From the website, customers will be able to purchase products through CreateSpace, Amazon, and Zazzle.

Marketing efforts will be conducted both online and off-line to drive traffic to the website. Online marketing efforts will include an active Facebook Fan Page, Twitter account, and YouTube channel. Off-line efforts will include sending the book to be reviewed by model railroad magazines and handing out flyers at train shows. Operations will be limited to one to two hours per week of marketing efforts along with evaluations of the current business strategy. The business is expected to break-even on its initial investment within the first year with sales potential of approximately $2000-$5000.

Products and Service

The Rockville Bridge will offer books, t-shirts, aprons, postcards, mugs, and a website as potential revenue sources.

The book, titled "90 Days to Rockville," will be a how-to guide for model railroaders interested in building a model of a stone arch bridge in similar style to Rockville Bridge. It will be a 150 page trade paperback printed in black and white on white paper. It will feature lots of photos and diagrams to explain the ideas behind the instructions in the book.

In addition to the book, several products will be made available featuring the bridge and the company logo. These items include a T-shirt, coffee mug, postcard, and apron.

The website will provide content about the bridge and models of the bridge. It will also be a platform for advertisers through Google Adsense and Amazon Affiliates services. The Amazon affiliates will be used to provide recommendations for books and products available from Amazon that will help the model builder build a model of Rockville Bridge. In addition, it will also direct traffic to the Amazon page for the "90 Days to Rockville" book.

Sales Channel

All books and products will be sold through online retailers. The products will be licensed to several print on-demand companies and royalties received for each sale made.

The book will be sold through CreateSpace, an Amazon company, specializing in print on-demand for books. The book will be available for sale through a CreateSpace website as well as be made available on Amazon.com. To allow for expanded distribution, we will pay the one time fee of $39 to upgrade to the Pro Plan offered by CreateSpace. This will allow the book to be listed by national book distributors as well as through Barnes and Noble Booksellers.

The remaining products will all be available for sale through Zazzle, a print on-demand company specializing in merchandise and apparel. All of these items will be available through our customized storefront page hosted by Zazzle.

Competition

There are a number of competitors for the business. This includes websites, books, and products that are similar to those planned to be offered.

There are numerous other model railroad and railfan websites that discuss Rockville Bridge. The largest, Railpictures.net, has hundreds of photos of the bridge.

While no modeling books about the bridge exist, Dan Cupper's book "Rails over the Susquehanna" offers a history of the bridge along with drawings of the bridge.

Since it is expected that the products offered by the company will appeal to those with an interest in the Pennsylvania Railroad, any suppliers, such as Historic Rail, of Pennsylvania Railroad apparel and mugs will be competitors.

Marketing and Sales Plan

A number of inexpensive online and offline promotions will be used to promote The Rockville Bridge. Online promotions will include setting up social networking accounts such as a Facebook Fan Page, Twitter account, and a YouTube Channel. The social networks will be used to stay in contact with followers of the site. Updates to each of the social networks should occur on the following schedule:

- ✓ Facebook Fan Page – One weekly status update. Should provide interesting content

relevant to Rockville Bridge such as links, photos, videos, and events.
- ✓ Twitter account – One weekly tweet of interesting content relevant to Rockville Bridge such as links, photos, videos, and events.
- ✓ YouTube Channel – Find and post interesting YouTube videos from Rockville Bridge. Should occur once or twice a month.

In addition, there are numerous websites devoted to links for model railroad hobbyist so the site will be listed with as many of them as possible. In addition, limited activity will be taken up on relevant message boards and communities.

There are several offline promotional activities that will be engaged. The book will be sent to the following magazines for review:

- ✓ Model Railroad News
- ✓ Railroad Model Craftsman
- ✓ Scale Rails

Also, a copy of the book will be sent to the Bridgeview Bed and Breakfast, which overlooks the bridge with a poster of the book for the owner to hang for guests to see.

Since a traveling model of the bridge was built, at every display that it is brought to, a copy of the book will be displayed and flyers will be handed out to people interested in purchasing the book.

There will be no paid advertising due to having such a small market for potential customers.

Operations

This business is intended to be worked on part-time. Therefore, it is expected that following the initial period of creating the products and building the website, approximately, one to two hours per week will be spent executing the marketing and sales plan and developing the future strategy.

Risks

There are several risks associated with this business that could stop it from having success. In no particular order they are:

- ✓ There is a very small market for the products, this may make it difficult to reach potential customers and generate sales.
- ✓ As a part time business, it may be difficult to respond to potential customers or issues in a

timely fashion resulting in poor customer experience
- ✓ Do not own domain www.rockvillebridge.com
- ✓ No plans for paid advertising could limit exposure for the website
- ✓ Problems with suppliers providing poor products or customer service
- ✓ Suppliers fail to pay

Financial Analysis and Projections

While this is a small company, it is important to understand the costs associated with the startup, breakeven point, and potential sales figures.

Startup costs will include several items. This includes the domain name and web hosting. In addition, proof copies of the book will need to purchase as well as some marketing expenses to mail copies of the book out for review and print a poster for the book. The startup expenses are listed below.

Startup Expenses	
Domain Name	$10
Web Hosting	75
Proof Copies of Book	22
Postage	30
Flyers	20
Total Expenses	$157

The company will be selling five different products, with seven different royalties. The book will be sold in three different channels, each of which has a different royalty. The remaining products will only be sold through Zazzle and have one royalty.

Product Royalties	
Book-Amazon	$9.32
Book-CreateSpace	13.31
Book-Wholesale	5.33
T-Shirt	2.30
Apron	2.00
Mug	2.39
Postcard	0.10

The most important financial projection to consider for such a small company is whether or not sales will cover the initial startup expenses and bring the company to break even. For this reason, included is a breakeven chart if there was only sales of the one item listed.

Breakeven Quantities		
Book-Amazon	$9.32	17
Book-CreateSpace	13.31	12
Book-Wholesale	5.33	30
T-Shirt	2.30	69
Apron	2.00	79
Mug	2.39	66
Postcard	0.10	1570

Resources
Additional Reading

This book is aimed at helping those interested in using the on-demand model as a basis for selling products. While this book will certainly provide you a good overview of business and marketing, it is certainly not complete. Here is a list of several other books I have found useful when either planning a business, running a business, or just plain needed motivation to keep going.

Start Up Advice
Lesonsky, Rieva, Start *Your Own Business*, Canada: Entrepreneur Press, 2004
Marketing
Levinson, Jay Conrad, *Guerilla Marketing*, Boston: Houghton Mifflin Company, 2007
Anderson, Chris, *Free – The Future of a Radical Price*, New York: Hyperion, 2007
Inspiration
Burlingham, Bo, *Small Giants – Companies that Choose to be Great Instead of Big*, New York: Penguin Group, 2005
Vaynerchuk, Gary, *Crush It!-Why Now is the Time to Cash in on Your Passion*, New York: HarperCollins, 2009

Resources
On-Demand Websites

This is a list of on-demand companies referenced in this book.

CaféPress
www.cafepress.com

CreateSpace
www.createspace.com

Lulu
www.lulu.com

Zazzle
www.zazzle.com

Google Adsense
www.google.com/adsense

Yahoo Publisher Network
publisher.yahoo.com

Commission Junction
www.cj.com

About the Author

Having built several successful on-demand businesses, Jim Spavins presents lessons learned and a practical step by step guide for enterprising content creators to get an on-demand business up off the ground. Jim is currently the Managing Principal at Isthmus Ventures, based in Madison, WI, which specializes in businesses using on-demand services.

Jim Spavins earned his Master's in Business Administration from the University of Wisconsin-Madison.

Business in Minutes Online

Looking for more? Have some questions about creating your business?

Visit us online at www.businessinminutes.com.

- ✓ Keep up to date with trends in the on-demand business world.
- ✓ Find links to companies offering services.
- ✓ See on-demand business success stories.

You will find all of this in a regularly updated blog. There are plenty of resources and links to everything you find in this book so you can easily access everything for yourself.

If you have a question you'd like answered or have a success story to share, send us an email at jim@businessinminutes.com.